A SERMON ON REGENERATION

A SERMON ON REGENERATION

By the

Rev. George Whitefield, M.A.

Late of Pembroke College, Oxford, and Chaplain to the Right Honorable the Countess of Huntingdon

CURIOSMITH

Minneapolis

2012

Published by Curiosmith.
P. O. Box 390293, Minneapolis, Minnesota, 55439.
Internet: curiosmith.com.
E-mail: shopkeeper@curiosmith.com.

Previously published—Boston: Re-printed by T. Fleet, for Charles
Harrison, over-against the Brazen Head in Cornhill, 1739.

The text of this edition is from *The Works of the Reverend George Whitefield*,
Vol. 6, Printed for EDWARD and CHARLES DILLY, in the Poultry; and Messrs.
KINCAID and CREECH, at Edinburgh. 1772.

The Outline of the Contents was added to this edition by the publisher.

ISBN 9781935626596

OUTLINE OF THE CONTENTS

A Sermon on Regeneration

A SERMON BY

George Whitefield, M.A.

If any man be in CHRIST, *he is a new creature.*
—2 CORINTHIANS 5:17.

The doctrine of our regeneration, or new birth in CHRIST JESUS, though one of the most fundamental doctrines of our holy religion; though so plainly and often pressed on us in sacred writ, "that he who runs may read;" nay though it is the very hinge on which the salvation of each of us turns, and a point too in which all sincere Christians, of every denomination, agree; yet it is so seldom considered, and so little experimentally understood by the generality of professors, that were we to judge of the truth of it, by the experience of most who call themselves Christians, we should be apt to imagine they had "not so much as heard" whether there be any such thing as regeneration or not. It is true, men for the most part are orthodox in the common articles of their creed; they believe "there is but one GOD, and one Mediator between GOD and men, even the man CHRIST JESUS;" and that there is no other name given under heaven, whereby they can be saved, besides his: But then tell them, they must be regenerated, they must be born again, they must be renewed in the very spirit, in the inmost faculties of their minds, ere they can truly call CHRIST, "Lord, Lord," or have an evidence that they have any share in the merits of his precious blood; and they are ready to cry out with *Nicodemus*, "How can these things be?" Or with the *Athenians*, on another occasion, "What will this babler say? he seemeth to be a setter-forth of strange doctrines;" because we preach unto them CHRIST, and the new-birth.

That I may therefore contribute my mite towards curing the fatal mistake of such persons, who would thus put asunder what GOD has inseparably joined together, and vainly think they are justified by CHRIST, or have their sins forgiven, and his perfect obedience imputed to them, when they are not sanctified, have not their natures changed, and made holy, I shall beg leave to enlarge on the words of the text in the following manner:

First, I shall endeavour to explain what is meant by being in CHRIST: "If any man be in CHRIST."

Secondly, What we are to understand by being a new creature: "If any man be in CHRIST he is a new creature."

Thirdly, I shall produce some arguments to make good the apostle's assertion. And

Fourthly, I shall draw some inferences from what may be delivered, and then conclude with a word or two of exhortation.

First, I am to endeavour to explain what is meant by this expression in the text, "If any man be in CHRIST."

Now a person may be said to be in CHRIST two ways. *First,* Only by an outward profession. And in this sense, every one that is called a Christian, or baptized into CHRIST's church, may be said to be in CHRIST. But that this is not the sole meaning of the apostle's phrase before us, is evident, because then, every one that names the name of CHRIST, or is baptized into his visible church, would be a new creature. Which is notoriously false, it being too plain, beyond all contradiction, that comparatively but few of those that are "born of water," are "born of the Spirit" likewise; to use another spiritual way of speaking, many are baptized with water, which were never baptized with the Holy Ghost.

To be in CHRIST therefore, in the full import of the word, must certainly mean something more than a bare outward profession, or being called after his name. For, as this same apostle tells us, "All are not *Israelites* that are of *Israel,*" so when applied to Christianity, all are not real Christians that are nominally such. Nay, this is so far from being the case, that our blessed LORD himself informs us, that many who have prophesied or preached in his name, and in his name cast out devils, and done many wonderful works, shall notwithstanding be dismissed at the last day, with "depart from me, I know you not, ye workers of iniquity."

It remains therefore, that this expression, "if any man be in CHRIST," must be understood in a

Second and closer signification, to be *in him* so as to partake of the benefits of his sufferings. To be in him not only by an outward profession, but by an inward change and purity of heart, and cohabitation of his Holy Spirit. To be in him, so as to be mystically united to him by a true and lively faith, and thereby to receive spiritual virtue from him, as the members of the natural body do from the head, or the branches from the vine. To be in him in such a manner as the apostle, speaking of himself, acquaints us he knew a person was, "I knew man in CHRIST," a true Christian; or, as he himself desires to be in CHRIST, when he wishes, in his epistle to the *Philippians*, that he might be found in him.

This is undoubtedly the proper meaning of the apostle's expression in the words of the text; so that what he says in his epistle to the *Romans* about circumcision, may very well be applied to the present subject; that he is not a real Christian who is only one outwardly; nor is that true baptism, which is only outward in the flesh. But he is a true Christian, who is one inwardly, whose baptism is that of the heart, in the Spirit, and not merely in the water, whose praise is not of man but of GOD. Or, as he speaketh in another place, "Neither circumcision nor uncircumcision availeth any thing (of itself) but a new creature." Which amounts to what he here declares in the verse now under consideration, that if any man be truly and properly in CHRIST, he is a new creature. Which brings me to show,

Secondly, What we are to understand by being a *new creature.*

And here it is evident at the first view, that this

expression is not to be so explained as though there was a physical change required to be made in us; or as though we were to be reduced to our primitive nothings, and then created and formed again. For, supposing we were, as *Nicodemus* ignorantly imagined, to enter a "second time into our mother's womb, and be born," alas! what would it contribute towards rendering us spiritually new creatures? Since "that which was born of the flesh would be flesh still;" we should be the same carnal persons as ever, being derived from carnal parents, and consequently receiving the seeds of all manner of sin and corruption from them. No, it only means, that we must be so altered as to the qualities and tempers of our minds, that we must entirely forget what manner of persons we once were. As it may be said of a piece of gold, that was once in the ore, after it has been cleansed, purified and polished, that it is a new piece of gold; as it may be said of a bright glass that has been covered over with filth, when it is wiped, and so become transparent and clear, that it is a new glass: Or, as it might be said of *Naaman*, when he recovered of his leprosy, and his flesh returned unto him like the flesh of a young child, that he was a new man; so our souls, though still the same as to essence, yet are so purged, purified and cleansed from their natural dross, filth and leprosy, by the blessed influences of the Holy Spirit, that they may be properly said to be made anew.

How this glorious change is wrought in the soul, cannot easily be explained: For no one knows the ways of the Spirit, save the Spirit of GOD himself. Not that this ought to be any argument against this doctrine; for, as our blessed LORD observed to *Nicodemus*, when he was discoursing on this very subject, "The wind bloweth where it listeth, and thou hearest the sound thereof, but knowest not whence it cometh and whither it goeth;" and if we are told of natural things, and we understand them not, how much less ought we to wonder, if we cannot immediately account for the invisible workings of the Holy Spirit? The truth of the matter is this: the doctrine of our regeneration, or new birth in CHRIST JESUS, is hard to be understood by the natural man. But that there is really such a thing, and that each of us must be spiritually born again, I shall endeavour to show under my

Third general head, in which I was to produce some arguments to make good the apostle's assertion.

And here one would think it sufficient to affirm,

First, That GOD himself, in his holy word, hath told us so. Many texts might be produced out of the Old Testament to prove this point, and indeed, one would wonder how *Nicodemus*, who was a teacher in *Israel*, and who was therefore to instruct the people in the spiritual meaning of the law, should be so ignorant of this grand article, as we find he really was, by his asking our blessed LORD, when he was pressing on him this topic, How can these things be? Surely, he could not forget how often the Psalmist had begged of GOD, to make him "a new heart," and "to renew a right spirit within him;" as likewise, how frequently the prophets had warned the people to make them "new hearts," and new minds, and so turn unto the LORD their GOD. But not to mention these and such like texts out of the Old Testament, this doctrine is so often and plainly repeated in the New, that, as I observed before, he who runs may read. For what says the great Prophet and Instructor of the world himself: "Except a man (every one that is naturally the offspring of *Adam*) be born again of water and the Spirit, he cannot enter into the kingdom of GOD." And lest we should be apt to slight this assertion, and *Nicodemus*-like, reject the doctrine, because we cannot immediately explain "How this thing can be;" our blessed Master therefore affirms it, as it were, by an oath, "Verily, verily, I say unto you," or, as it may be read, I the Amen; I, who am truth itself, say unto you, that it is the unalterable appointment of my heavenly Father, that "unless a man be born again, he cannot enter into the kingdom of GOD."

Agreeable to this, are those many passages we meet with in the epistles, where we are commanded to be "renewed in the Spirit," or, which was before explained, in the inmost faculties of our minds; to "put off the Old Man, which is corrupt; and to put on the New Man, which is created after GOD, in righteousness and true holiness;" that "old things must pass away, and that all things must become new;" that we are to be "saved by the washing of regeneration, and the renewing of the Holy Ghost." Or, methinks, was there no other passage to be produced besides the words of the text, it would be full enough, since the apostle therein positively affirms, that "If any man be in CHRIST, he is a *new creature.*"

Now, what can be understood by all these different terms of being *born again*, of *putting off the Old Man*, and *putting on the New*, of being *renewed in the Spirit of our minds*, and becoming *new creatures;* but that Christianity requires a thorough, real inward change of heart? Do we think these, and such-like forms of speaking, are mere metaphors, words of a bare sound, without any real solid signification? Indeed, it is to be feared, some men would have them interpreted so; but alas! unhappy men! they are not to be envied in their metaphorical interpretation: it will be well, if they do not interpret themselves out of their salvation.

Multitudes of other texts might be produced to confirm this same truth; but those already quoted are so plain and convincing, that one would imagine no one should deny it; were we not told, there are some, "who having eyes, see not, and ears, hear not, and that will not understand with their hearts, or hear with their ears, lest they should be converted, and CHRIST should heal them."

But I proceed to a

Second argument; and that shall be taken from the purity of GOD, and the present corrupt and polluted state of man.

God is described in holy scripture (and I speak to those who profess to know the scripture) as a Spirit; as a being of such infinite sanctity, as to be of "purer eyes than to behold iniquity;" as to be so transcendently holy, that it is said "the very heavens are not clean in his sight; and the angels themselves he chargeth with folly." On the other hand, man is described (and every regenerate person will find it true by his own experience) as a creature altogether "conceived and born in sin;" as having "no good thing dwelling in him;" as being "carnal, sold under sin;" nay, as having "a mind which is at enmity with GOD," and suchlike. And since there is such an infinite disparity, can any one conceive how a filthy, corrupted, polluted wretch can dwell with an infinitely pure and holy GOD, before he is changed, and rendered, in some measure, like him? Can he, who is of purer eyes than to behold iniquity, dwell with it? Can he, in whose sight the heavens are not clean, delight to dwell with uncleanness itself? No, we might as well suppose light to have communion with darkness, or CHRIST to have concord with *Belial*. But I pass on to a

Third argument, which shall be founded on the consideration of the nature of that happiness GOD has prepared for those that unfeignedly love him.

To enter indeed on a minute and particular description of heaven, would be vain and presumptuous, since we are told that "eye hath not seen, nor ear heard, neither hath it entered into the heart of man to conceive, the things that are there prepared" for the sincere followers of the holy JESUS, even in this life, much less in that which is to come. However, this we may venture to affirm in general, that as GOD is a Spirit, so the happiness he has laid up for his people is spiritual likewise; and consequently, unless our carnal minds are changed, and spiritualized, we can never be made meet to partake of that inheritance with the saints in light.

It is true, we may flatter ourselves, that, supposing we continue in our natural corrupt estate, and carry all our lusts along with us, we should, notwithstanding, relish heaven, was GOD to admit us therein. And so we might, was it a *Mahometan* paradise, wherein we were to take our full swing in sensual delights. But since its joys are only spiritual, and no unclean thing can possibly enter those blessed mansions, there is an absolute necessity of our being changed, and undergoing a total renovation of our depraved natures, before we can have any taste or relish of those heavenly pleasures.

It is, doubtless, for this reason, that the apostle declares it to be the irrevocable decree of the Almighty, that "without holiness, (without being made pure by regeneration, and having the image of GOD thereby reinstamped upon the soul) no man shall see the LORD." And it is very observable, that our divine Master, in the famous passage before referred to, concerning the absolute necessity of regeneration, does not say, Unless a man be born again, he *shall not*, but "unless a man be born again, he *cannot* enter into the kingdom of GOD." It is founded in the very nature of things, that unless we have dispositions wrought in us suitable to the objects that are to entertain us, we can take no manner of complacency or satisfaction in them. For instance; what delight can the most harmonious music afford to a deaf, or what pleasure can the most excellent picture give to a blind man? Can a tasteless palate relish the richest dainties, or a filthy swine be pleased with the finest garden of flowers? No: and what reason can be assigned for it? An answer is ready; because they have neither of them any tempers of mind correspondent or agreeable to what they are to be diverted with. And thus it is with the soul hereafter: for death makes no more alteration in the soul, than as it enlarges its faculties, and makes it capable of receiving deeper impressions either of pleasure or pain. If it delighted to converse with GOD here, it will be transported with the sight of his glorious Majesty hereafter. If it was pleased with the communion of saints on earth, it will be infinitely more so with the communion and society of holy angels, and the spirits of just men made perfect in heaven. But if the opposite of all this be true, we may assure ourselves the soul could not be happy, was GOD himself to admit it (which he never will do) into the regions of the blessed. But it is time for me to hasten to the

Fourth argument, because CHRIST's redemption will not be complete in us, unless we are new creatures.

If we reflect indeed on the first and chief end of our blessed LORD's coming, we shall find it was to be a propitiation for our sins, to give his life a ransom for many. But then, if the benefits of our dear Redeemer's death were to extend no farther than barely to procure forgiveness of our sins, we should have as little reason to rejoice in it, as a poor condemned criminal that is ready to perish by some fatal disease, would have in receiving a pardon from his judge. For Christians would do well to consider, that there is not only a legal hindrance to our happiness, as we are breakers of GOD's law, but also a moral impurity in our natures, which renders us incapable of enjoying heaven (as hath been already proved) till some mighty change have been wrought in us. It is necessary therefore, in order to make CHRIST's redemption complete, that we should have a grant of GOD's Holy Spirit to change our natures, and so prepare us for the enjoyment of that happiness our Saviour has purchased by his precious blood.

Accordingly the holy scriptures inform us, that whom CHRIST justifies, or whose sins he forgives, and to whom he imputes his perfect obedience, those he also sanctifies, purifies and cleanses, and totally changeth their corrupted natures. As the scripture also speaketh in another place, "CHRIST is to us justification, sanctification, and then redemption." But,

Fourthly, Proceed we now to the next general thing proposed, to draw some inferences from what has been delivered. And,

First, If he that is in CHRIST be a new creature, this may serve as a reproof for those who rest in a bare performance of outward duties, without perceiving any real inward change of heart.

We may observe a great many persons to be very punctual in the regular returns of public and private prayer, as likewise of receiving the holy communion, and perhaps now and then too in keeping a fast. But here is the misfortune, they rest barely in the use of the means, and think all is over, when they have thus complied with those sacred institutions; whereas, were they rightly informed, they would consider, that all the instituted means of grace, as prayer, fasting, hearing and reading the word of GOD, receiving the blessed sacrament, and such-like, are no farther serviceable to us, than as they are found to make us inwardly better, and to carry on the spiritual life in the soul.

It is true, they are means; but then they are only means; they are part, but not the whole of religion: for if so, who more religious than the Pharisee? He fasted twice in the week, and gave tithes of all that he possessed, and yet was not justified, as our Saviour himself informs us, in the sight of GOD.

You perhaps, like the Pharisee, may fast often, and make long prayers; you may, with *Herod*, hear good sermons gladly. But yet, if you continue vain and trifling, immoral or worldly-minded, and differ from the rest of your neighbours barely in going to church, or in complying with some outward performances, are you better than they? No, in no wise; you are by far much worse; for if you use them, and at the same time abuse them, you thereby encourage others to think there is nothing in them, and therefore must expect to receive the greater damnation. But,

Secondly, If he that is *in* CHRIST be a new creature, then this may check the groundless presumption of another class of professors, who rest in the attainment of some moral virtues, and falsely imagine they are good Christians if they are just in their dealings, temperate in their diet, and do no hurt or violence to any man.

But if this was all that is requisite to make us

Christians, why might not the heathens of old be good Christians, who were remarkable for these virtues? or St. *Paul* before his conversion, who tells us, that he lived in all good conscience? but we find he renounces all dependence on works of this nature, and only desires to be found in CHRIST, and to know the power of his resurrection, or have an experimental proof of receiving the Holy Ghost, purchased for him by the death, and ensured and applied to him by the resurrection of JESUS CHRIST.

The sum of the matter is this: Christianity includes morality, as grace does reason; but if we are only mere Moralists, if we are not inwardly wrought upon, and changed by the powerful operations of the Holy Spirit, and our moral actions, proceed from a principle of a new nature, however we may call ourselves Christians, we shall be found naked at the great day, and in the number of those, who have neither CHRIST's righteousness imputed to them for their justification in the sight, nor holiness enough in their souls as the consequence of that, in order to make them meet for the enjoyment, of GOD. Nor,

Thirdly, Will this doctrine less condemn those, who rest in a partial amendment of themselves, without experiencing a thorough, real, inward change of heart.

A little acquaintance with the world will furnish us with instances, of no small number of persons, who, perhaps, were before openly profane; but seeing the ill consequences of their vices, and the many worldly inconveniencies it has reduced them to, on a sudden, as it were, grow civilized; and thereupon flatter themselves that they are very religious, because they differ a little from their former selves, and are not so scandalously wicked as once they were: whereas, at the same time, they shall have some secret darling sin or other, some beloved *Dalilah* or *Herodias,* which they will not part with; some hidden lust, which they will not mortify; some vicious habit, which they will not take pains to root out. But wouldst thou know, O vain man! whoever thou art, what the LORD thy GOD requires of thee? thou must be informed, that nothing short of a thorough sound conversion will fit thee for the kingdom of heaven. It is not enough to turn from profaneness to civility; but thou must turn from civility to godliness. Not only some, but "all things must become new" in thy soul. It will profit thee but little to do many things, if yet some one thing thou lackest. In short, thou must not only be an almost, but altogether a new creature, or in vain thou boasteth that thou art a Christian.

Fourthly, If he that is in CHRIST be a new creature, then this may be prescribed as an infallible rule for every person of whatever denomination, age, degree or quality, to judge himself by; this being the only solid foundation, whereon we can build a well-grounded assurance of pardon, peace, and happiness.

We may indeed depend on the broken reed of an external profession; we may think we are good enough, if we lead such sober, honest, moral lives, as many heathens did. We may imagine we are in a safe condition, if we attend on the public offices of religion, and are constant in the duties of our closets. But unless all these tend to reform our lives, and change our hearts, and are only used as so many channels of divine grace; as I told you before, so I tell you again, Christianity will profit you nothing.

Let each of us therefore seriously put this question to our hearts: Have we received the Holy Ghost since we believed? Are we new creatures in CHRIST, or no? At least, if we are not so yet, is it our daily endeavour to become such? Do we constantly and conscientiously use all the means of grace required thereto? Do we fast, watch and pray? Do we, not lazily seek, but laboriously strive to enter in at the strait gate? In short, do we renounce our own righteousness, take up our crosses and follow CHRIST? If so, we are in that narrow way which leads to life; the good seed is sown in our hearts, and will, if duly watered and nourished by a regular persevering use of all the means of grace, grow up to eternal life. But on the contrary, if we have only heard, and know not experimentally, whether there be any Holy Ghost; if we are strangers to fasting, watching and prayer, and all the other spiritual exercises of devotion; if we are content to go in the broad way, merely because we see most other people do so, without once reflecting whether it be the right one or not; in short, if we are strangers, nay enemies to the cross of CHRIST, by lives of worldly-mindedness, and sensual pleasure, and thereby make others think, that Christianity is but an empty name, a bare formal profession; if this be the case, I say, CHRIST is as yet dead in vain, to us; we are under the guilt of our sins; and are unacquainted with a true and thorough conversion.

But beloved, I am persuaded better things of you, and things that accompany salvation, though I thus speak; I would humbly hope that you are sincerely persuaded, that he who hath not the Spirit of CHRIST is none of his; and that, unless the Spirit, which raised JESUS from the dead, dwell in you here, neither will your mortal bodies be quickened by the same Spirit to dwell with him hereafter.

Let me therefore (as was proposed in the *last* place) earnestly exhort you, in the name of our LORD JESUS CHRIST, to act suitable to those convictions, and to live as Christians, that are commanded in holy writ, to "put off their former conversation concerning the Old Man, and to put on the New Man, which is created after GOD in righteousness and true holiness."

It must be owned indeed, that this is a great and difficult work; but, blessed be GOD, it is not impossible. Many thousands of happy souls have been assisted by a divine power to bring it about, and why should we despair of success? Is GOD's hand shortened, that it cannot save? Was he the GOD of our Fathers, is he not the GOD of their children also? Yes, doubtless, of their children also. It is a task likewise, that will put us to some pain; it will oblige us to part with some lust, to break with some friend, to mortify some beloved passion, which may be exceeding dear to us, and perhaps as hard to leave, as to cut off a right-hand, or pluck out a right-eye. But what of all this? Will not the being made a real living member of CHRIST, a child of GOD, and an inheritor of the kingdom of heaven, abundantly make amends for all this trouble? Undoubtedly it will.

The setting about and carrying on this great and necessary work, perhaps may, nay assuredly will expose us also to the ridicule of the unthinking part of mankind, who will wonder, that we run not into the same excess of riot with themselves; and because we deny our sinful appetites, and are not conformed to this world, being commanded in scripture to do the one, and to have our conversation in heaven, in opposition to the other, they may count our lives folly, and our end to be without honour. But will not the being numbered among the saints, and shining as the stars for ever and ever, be a more than sufficient recompense for all the ridicule, calumny, or reproach, we can possibly meet with here?

Indeed, was there no other reward attended a thorough conversion, but that peace of GOD, which is the unavoidable consequence of it, and which, even in this life, "passeth all understanding," we should have great reason to rejoice. But when we consider, that this is the least of those mercies GOD has prepared for those that are in CHRIST, and become new creatures; that, this is but the beginning of an eternal succession of pleasures; that the day of our deaths, which the unconverted, unrenewed sinner must so much dread, will be, as it were, but the first day of our new births, and open to us an everlasting scene of happiness and comfort; in short, if we remember, that they who are regenerate and born again, have a real title to all the glorious promises of the gospel, and are infallibly certain of being as happy, both here and hereafter, as an all-wise, all-gracious, all-powerful GOD can make them; methinks, every one that has but the least concern for the salvation of his precious and immortal soul, having such promises, such an hope, such an eternity of happiness set before him, should never cease watching, praying, and striving, till he find a real, inward, saving change wrought in his heart, and thereby doth know of a truth, that he dwells in CHRIST, and CHRIST in him; that he is a new creature, therefore a child of GOD; that he is already an inheritor, and will ere long be an actual possessor of the kingdom of heaven.

Which GOD of his infinite mercy grant, through JESUS CHRIST our LORD. To whom, etc.

NOTES

NOTES

MAN'S QUESTIONS & GOD'S ANSWERS

Am I accountable to God?
"Every one of us shall give account of himself to God." (Romans 14:12).

Has God seen all my ways?
"All things are naked and opened unto the eyes of Him with whom we have to do." (Hebrews 4:13).

Does He charge me with sin?
"The Scripture hath concluded all under sin." (Galatians 3:22).
"All have sinned." (Romans 3:23).

Will He punish sin?
"The soul that sinneth, it shall die." (Ezekiel 18:4).
"For the wages of sin is death." (Romans 6:23).

Must I perish?
"God is not willing that any perish, but that all should come to repentance." (2 Peter 3:9).

How can I escape?
"Believe on the Lord Jesus Christ, and thou shalt be saved." (Acts 16:31).

Is He able to save me?
"He is able also to save them to the uttermost that come unto God by Him." (Hebrews 7:25).

Is He willing?
"Christ Jesus came into the world to save sinners." (1 Timothy 1:15).

Am I saved on believing?
"He that believeth on the Son hath everlasting life." (John 3:36).

Can I be saved now?
"Now is the accepted time; behold, now is the day of salvation." (2 Corinthians 6:2).

As I am?
"Him that cometh to Me I will in no wise cast out." (John 6:37).

Shall I not fall away?
"Him that is able to keep you from falling." (Jude 24).

If saved, how should I live?
"They which live should not henceforth live unto themselves, but unto Him which died for them." (2 Corinthians 5:15).

What about death, and eternity?
"I go to prepare a place for you; that where I am, there ye may be also." (John 14:2, 3).

www.ingramcontent.com/pod-product-compliance
Lightning Source LLC
Chambersburg PA
CBHW032115040426
42337CB00041B/1466